ISBN: 9781649696632

Cruelty - Free Is The Way to Be!
by Sabrina Fair Andronica

Have you ever noticed a bunny on the label of a bar of soap or any other item? This means these products are free from animal testing! In this book you'll hear from the little guy himself and meet his other friends. Brooks the Bunny is here to guide the next generation to shop consciously, and compassionately, with educational facts and fun tips! These brands not only save animals' lives but many of them are also eco-friendly, free of chemicals and toxins, and use less plastic. By supporting cruelty-free companies, you're living greener, improving you and your family's health, and saving the planet!

Printed in the United States of America

THIS BOOK BELONGS TO

_____

DEDICATION:

TO MY BETTER HALF, BROOKS CROUSE. HE'S THE ONE WHO HAS GUIDED ME TO LIVE A CRUELTY-FREE LIFE STYLE.

TO CHRIS DEROSE, FOUNDER OF LAST CHANCE FOR ANIMALS - A NONPROFIT ORGANIZATION KNOWN FOR ITS INVESTIGATIONS AGAINST ANIMAL TESTING SINCE 1984.

TO THE TWO ANIMAL ACTIVISTS WHO RAISED ME. MAY MY PRECIOUS MOTHER ALWAYS WATCH OVER ME.

A REGULAR PORTION OF THE PROCEEDS WILL GO TO "MOM AND POP" ANIMAL RESCUES WHO TRULY HELP THOSE IN NEED.

HELLO!
I'M BROOKS
THE BUNNY!
MY FRIEND
MEG THINKS
I'M CUTE AND
FUNNY!

The Stump-tailed macaque may be hunted by different animals, but humans are their biggest predators. Instead of living in their natural habitat, many are in research laboratories. They're considered a vulnerable species and could possibly go extinct during this century.

THIS IS MY FRIEND, MEG THE MONKEY. SHE IS SUPER SMART AND SPUNKY!

7

SPEAKING OF MY FRIENDS, LET ME INTRODUCE YOU TO THE REST! THEY ARE FUN, SWEET, LOYAL AND JUST THE BEST!

THIS IS MY
FRIEND, BILLY
THE BEAGLE.
HE'S VERY
PEACEFUL AND
LOVES PEOPLE.

A genetic mutation that occurred in a laboratory in 1978 resulted in Skinny pigs. This hairless breed is generally used today in dermatology studies, since their skin is more sensitive than haired Guinea pigs.

THIS IS MY FRIEND, GIO THE GUINEA PIG. HE MAY BE SMALL, BUT HIS HEART'S REALLY BIG!

AND LASTLY MY FRIEND, KAIA THE KITTY. SHE IS SO CUDDLY AND PRETTY.

BUT FRIENDS LIKE MINE AREN'T ALWAYS TOGETHER AND FREE. THEY TEST PRODUCTS ON US AND THEN THROW AWAY THE KEY.

Not Tested On Animals

Coloured
Pencils

4109 450204

CRUELTY
FREE

Mentha piperita	
Ocimum sanctum	10 mg
Curcuma amada	5.0 mg
Curcuma longa	2.0 mg
Aloe barbadensis	2.0 mg
Borax (Purified)	2.0 mg

4904109450204

24

MY FRIENDS THANK YOU AND YOURS FOR SHOPPING CRUELTY-FREE! YOUR KIND CHOICES ALLOW US TO JUST BE!

THE HOPE ALTERNATIVE TESTING BRINGS!

ANIMAL TESTING IS HUMAN GUESSING! EVERY YEAR ALL OVER THE WORLD, OVER 115 MILLION ANIMALS ARE USED IN RESEARCH, YET 90% OF DRUGS FAIL IN HUMAN TRIALS BECAUSE ANIMALS ARE BIOLOGICALLY DIFFERENT. FOR OVER A CENTURY, THIS BARBARIC PRACTICE HAS NOT PRODUCED RELIABLE CURES. EVEN SO, ITS USE CONTINUES BECAUSE OF FINANCIAL GAIN AND THE REFERENCE OF PAST EXPERIMENTS.

THE GOOD NEWS IN ALL OF THIS? THERE IS A GAME-CHANGING SCIENCE THAT EXISTS AND NO LONGER REQUIRES PAINFUL SKIN AND INGESTION TESTS TO BE FORCED ON A FRIGHTENED BROOKS AND GIO. WITH TODAY'S TECHNOLOGY, MODERN COMPANIES PRACTICE ALTERNATIVE TESTING THAT IMPROVES THE QUALITY AND THE ETHICS OF SCIENCE, WITHOUT PUTTING HUMANS AND ANIMALS AT RISK. FOR EXAMPLE, HUMAN AND ANIMAL CELLS CAN BE GROWN IN A LABORATORY AND CULTIVATED INTO A 3D STRUCTURE OF MINIATURE ORGANS THAT CAN BE USED TO APPROVE NEW DRUGS AND CHEMICALS.

IMAGINE 10,000 CHIPS TAKING THE SPACE OF ONE CAGE WITH FAR MORE ACCURATE RESULTS THAN WITH OUTDATED ANIMAL TESTING. LET'S REMIND THESE COMPANIES, AND PROVE TO THE OTHERS, WHY WE THINK SHOPPING CRUELTY-FREE IS THE WAY TO BE!

ABOUT THE AUTHOR

As a young girl I showed a keen interest in writing. At seven I wrote my first screenplay with the help of my screenwriting father. The following year The Los Angeles Times published a Kids' Reading Page to promote literacy before age nine and my little fun submissions about animals were chosen twice. I hope to share with children all over the world my life passion for animal activism and to inspire them with stories of love and compassion. Be sure to check out my first book, Adventure At Rainbow Bridge, a story meant to help families cope with the loss of a pet.

 @alwaysfairbooks

Books available on Amazon.com

alwaysfairbooks@gmail.com

ABOUT THE ILLUSTRATOR

"When I was a little girl, I "lived" in the fabulous drawings of my grandfather. He was an artist. I dreamed of learning to draw the same colorful, attractive and funny illustrations. I am very glad that my dream came true and I can delight children and their parents with my drawings.

Believe in your dreams! Welcome to my world!"

 @ SKlakina

Portfolio: www.behance.net/SKlakina

sklakina@gmail.com

Books available on Amazon.com

HERE IS A PHOTO OF THE AUTHOR, SABRINA FAIR ANDRONICA, HANGING OUT WITH TWO REAL LIFE SURVIVORS! MEET LORETTA THE BUNNY AND CALLIE THE BEAGLE. THEY WERE EACH RESCUED AND REHABILITATED FROM YEARS OF LIVING IN LABORATORIES, THANKS TO THE AMAZING ORGANIZATION, BEAGLE FREEDOM PROJECT. NOW THEY ARE ENJOYING THE GOOD LIFE WITH A LOT OF SUNSHINE AND LOVING HANDS. #RESCUEREHABREPEAT

Cruelty-Cutter App

THERE WILL BE TIMES THAT CRUELTY-FREE PRODUCTS WON'T HAVE BROOKS THE BUNNY ON IT. THAT'S WHERE THE CRUELTY-CUTTER APP COMES IN! DOWNLOAD THE FREE APP AND SCAN BARCODES TO LEARN WHAT PRODUCTS ARE TESTED ON ANIMALS. IF A PRODUCT IS NOT CRUELTY-FREE, YOU CAN "BITE BACK" AND HAVE THE OPTION TO SHARE IT WITH OTHERS, BOYCOTT THE BRAND OR CHECK OUT A LIST OF CRUELTY-FREE ALTERNATIVES. IF IT IS CRUELTY-FREE, YOU CAN ADD IT TO YOUR FAVORITES OR CLICK ON A DIRECT LINK TO THE PRODUCT'S WEBSITE. BY TAKING ACTION IN ANY OF THE WAYS MENTIONED ABOVE, YOU GAIN DOGGIE DOLLARS THAT CAN BE REDEEMED FOR DISCOUNTS AND SPECIAL PROMOTIONS ON CRUELTY-FREE PRODUCTS FROM CRUELTY-CUTTER'S MONTHLY SPONSORS! THIS APP IS THE MOST CURRENT AND DILIGENT CRUELTY-FREE LIST ON THE RADAR, AND IS DIRECTLY LINKED TO BEAGLE FREEDOM PROJECT. THEY RESCUE BEAGLES AND OTHER ANIMALS USED FOR ANIMAL EXPERIMENTATION IN RESEARCH LABORATORIES, GIVING THEM A CHANCE AT LIFE IN A LOVING HOME.

YOU CAN FOLLOW THEM ON INSTAGRAM:
@BEAGLEFREEDOM
@CRUELTYCUTTER

Q&A:

1. DID BROOKS THE BUNNY AND HIS FRIENDS INSPIRE YOU TO SHOP CRUELTY-FREE AND CONSCIOUSLY?

2. HOW WOULD YOU MAKE OTHERS AWARE OF KINDER PRODUCTS?

3. WHAT IS ONE WAY YOU WOULD SPREAD YOUR COMPASSION WITH THE WORLD?

WE LOVE YOU!

CPSIA information can be obtained
at www.ICGtesting.com
Printed in the USA
BVHW022307040521
606413BV00009B/425